Ideas for music-making with very young children

Written by
Anice Paterson and David Wheway

Illustrations by Isabel Barnbrook

LITTLE BOOKS WITH BIG IDEAS

Reprinted 2009, 2011
Published 2009 by A&C Black Publishers Limited
36 Soho Square, London W1D 3QY
www.acblack.com

First published 2003 by Featherstone Education Limited

ISBN 978-1-9041-8754-7

Text © Anice Paterson and David Wheway 2003
Illustrations © Isabel Barnbrook 2003
Series Editor Sally Featherstone

A CIP record for this publication is available from the British Library.

All rights reserved. No part of this publication may be reproduced in any form or by any means - graphic, electronic, or mechanical, including photocopying, recording, taping or information storage or retrieval systems - without the prior permission in writing of the publishers.

Printed in Great Britain by Latimer Trend & Company Limited

This book is produced using paper that is made from wood grown in managed, sustainable forests. It is natural, renewable and recyclable. The logging and manufacturing processes conform to the environmental regulations of the country of origin.

To see our full range of titles
visit www.acblack.com

Contents

Focus of the page	pages
Introduction	4-5
Music and learning: Enjoying and being confident with music	6-7
Section 1 (Movement)	9
Shake it around	10-11
The key to it all	12-13
What a character	14-15
Keep it still	16-17
Section 2 (Body sounds)	19
Hands	20-21
Feet	22-23
Mouths	24-25
Section 3 (Using voices)	27
Sing lots of songs	28-29
Sing the register	30-31
Teddy Bear, Teddy Bear	32-33
Move along please	34-35
Choral speaking	36-37
Tones	38-39
Section 4 (Using other sound sources and instruments)	41
Making your own instruments	42-43
Get co-ordinated	44-45
Let sleeping bells lie	46-47
How long does it last?	48-49
I went to market	50-51
What's different?	52-53
Section 5 (Patterns and numbers)	55
Five Green Bottles	56-57
Do it again	58-59
Birds, beasts and butterflies	60-61
Section 6 (Rhymes and stories)	63
What's your name again?	64-65
Grandfather, father and son	66-67
Animal fair	68-69
Peace at last!	70-71
Goldilocks	72-73
Story trails	74-76
Additional resources	77

Introduction

The activities in this Little Book build on many that will already be familiar in settings. They have been chosen as they show the contributions that music can make to children's experiences, and the relationship between music and other areas of a child's development; in particular literacy, numeracy, physical coordination, collaboration, concentration and confidence building.

On each page you will find:

1. Clearly identified **learning intentions** from the Early Learning Goals in Knowledge and Understanding of the World
2. **Musical concepts** and other learning being addressed or established during the activity
3. **Key vocabulary** for the activity (useful for you and other adults in your team)
4. **Resources** needed and the ideal layout for the space and equipment used
5. **Instructions** that will guide you through the activity.

There is considerable emphasis on movement as a way of internalising a sense of pulse and developing feelings in response to music. Developing children's listening skills clearly has a vital role in their learning elsewhere and all activities provide opportunities for careful listening.

Enjoying music with young children

Making music does not always depend on access to instruments. Clapping or tapping a rhythm on your knees or a table provides a perfectly good basis for the children to dance to. Also don't expect 'perfect' singing. Children need a long time to develop their vocal chords so that they can sing in tune. The important things are participation and enjoyment.

Where instruments are used, it is very important that children get used to hearing good quality sound from the outset. Establish some simple ground rules to help children manage instruments without unacceptable levels of noise for others in the building, and be consistent in how you apply them.

The Early Learning Goals

The Early Learning Goals for musical learning and appreciation appear in many places in the Foundation Stage curriculum.

In **Creative Development** they will:
- recognise and explore how sounds can be changed, sing simple songs from memory, recognise repeated sounds and sound patterns, and match movements to music;
- use their imagination in music, dance, imaginative play and stories;
- respond in a variety of ways to what they hear;
- express and communicate their ideas, thoughts and feelings by using a variety of songs and instruments.

In **Social Development** (where children learn to work together, share and co-operate) they will:
- be confident to try new activities, initiate ideas and speak in a familiar group;
- maintain attention, concentration and sit quietly when appropriate;
- work as part of a group or class, taking turns and sharing fairly;
- select and use activities and resources independently.

In **Communication, Language and Literacy** they will:
- interact with others, negotiating plans and activities, and taking turns in conversations;
- sustain attentive listening, responding to what they have heard by relevant comments, questions or actions;
- listen with enjoyment and respond to stories, songs and other music, rhymes and poems and make up their own stories, rhymes and poems;
- use language to imagine and recreate roles and experiences;
- use talk to organise, sequence and clarify thinking, ideas, feelings and events.

In **Mathematical Development** they will:
- talk about, recognise and recreate simple patterns.

In **Physical Development** they will:
- move with imagination;
- move with control and co-ordination;
- show awareness of space, of themselves and others;
- use a range of small and large equipment.

Music and learning

There is a growing body of evidence that shows that music can help young children to learn. Even before birth, a baby can hear voices, music and sounds, and comes to recognise the voices of their family and the sounds of their home. Babies respond to **all** kinds of music. They particularly respond to the sort of music their mother likes and listens to, and will continue to react to this familiar music after birth.

Making and listening to music uses both sides of the brain, and responding to music uses both sides of the body. Clapping, stamping, walking, jumping, skipping, dancing and playing simple instruments also stimulate the whole brain, particularly when children use both hands, both feet and both sides of their bodies.

Enjoying and being confident with music

Practitioners are often anxious about providing musical experiences for the children they work with. Some think that they need perfect pitch and an ability to play tuned instruments. This is not true!

The secret of successful music-making with children is to relax and enjoy yourself; if you are having fun, the children will have fun too. If you play the music and sing the songs you like, they will join in and sing along with you. Encourage children to be inventive with sounds, to use different voices in stories, to sing as they work and play, and to use sound makers as naturally as they use scissors and paint brushes.

In this way music will become a natural part of your setting, not a specialist activity taught by specialist adults at particular times in particular places.

Ten top tips for successful music:

1. Relax and enjoy it.
2. Play music at all times of the day, not just in music sessions.
3. Play all sorts of music.
4. Use different voices when you tell stories.
5. Encourage the children to talk, sing make sounds as they work and play.
6. Play listening games and make sure children know when it is 'listening time'.
7. Movement adds power to music and reinforces learning. Using both hands or both feet is particularly effective.
8. Sound-makers don't have to be expensive. Homemade and found items are just as good.
9. Work on rhythm: clapping, tapping, slapping, stamping, marching, clicking and patting.
10. The model you provide as a music-maker is important.

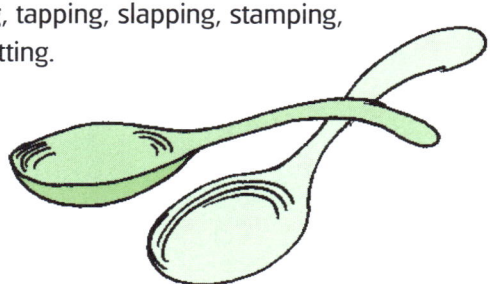

◆ Section 1

Physical response to music happens from birth, and recent research indicates that the unborn child is also affected by music heard in the womb. Movement is the most natural way to respond to music and to show the feelings it induces.

Activities in this section will help children to:

- ▶ respond to sounds
- ▶ develop feeling responses
- ▶ listen acutely
- ▶ develop good co-ordination.

Shake it around

Knowledge and concepts

Early Learning Goals:
Move with control and co-ordination
Match movements to music

Concepts and other learning:
Develop a feeling for the qualities of sounds
Respond to sounds with body movements

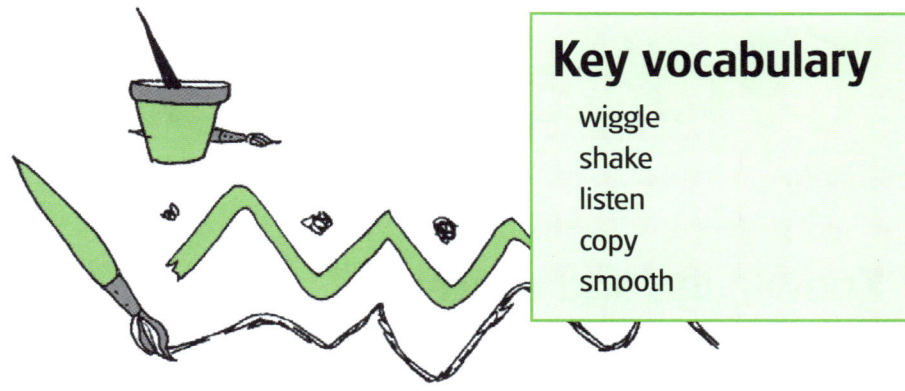

Key vocabulary
wiggle
shake
listen
copy
smooth

Resources and layout

▶ 3 or 4 distinctive instrumental sounds e.g. shaking tambourine, tapping drum, vibra slap and xylophone
▶ space for the children to move around

Activity

1. **Play** each sound to the children and ask them to show how it makes them move.
2. **Pick** three or four good moves and agree and practice the actions for everyone e.g.
    * shaking tambourine – shake hands in the air
    * tapping drum – tiptoe around the room
    * vibra slap – wiggle the whole body
    * running up the xylophone – swimming smoothly around the room.
3. **Play** the sounds in different sequences and children move and respond accurately to the sounds.

and something else
Children could paint or draw 'in time':
✔ **Tapping** a drum might produce a 'dotty' picture
✔ **Shaking** a tambourine might produce a zigzag picture.

The key to it all

Knowledge and concepts

Early Learning Goals:
Move with control and co-ordination
Match movements to music

Concepts and other learning:
Respond to a sound, reflecting on the quality of the sound
Listen carefully

Key vocabulary

loud   regular
soft   pattern
long
short

Resources and layout

▶ a bulky set of keys that makes a good noise
▶ children sitting on the carpet

Activity

1. **Everyone** holds their arms out in front and wiggles their fingers.
2. **Shake** the keys and ask everyone to wiggle their fingers when the keys are shaken.
3. **Shake** the keys in a variety of ways e.g. vigorously, gently, for a long time, for a short time, in a regular pattern etc. The children move their fingers in a way that reflects the way the sound is made.

and something else

✔ **Try** it behind a screen or desk so that they have to respond to the sound, not the visual stimulus.
✔ **Let** some children lead with the keys.

What a character

Knowledge and concepts
Early Learning Goals:
Sustain attentive listening
Respond to music and move with confidence

Concepts and other learning:
Reflect on the quality of a sound, and move in response to it

Key vocabulary

strong   listen
loud   mood
procession
ceremony

Resources and layout

▶ recorded music with a strong character e.g. brass band marching, floating electronic music or flute
Maximum 2 minutes per extract

▶ sitting in a circle to start, but with space to move around

Activity

1. **All** listen to one piece of music. Children just move while they sit to get the feel of it. Don't encourage big movements at this point.
2. **Talk** about words that describe the music – strong, bouncy, floaty etc.
3. **Talk** about the context of the music – music for out of doors, for processions, for soldiers, for skating etc.
4. **Choose** a suitable event for the music and let the children process or skate or march.
5. **Try** the same thing with another contrasting piece.

and something else

✔ **March,** float, skate or process in twos, fours or even eights. Talk about directions, mood and the shapes made.
What is the mood of the people? Are they happy, sad or serious?

✔ **Try** singing a bit of the music now they have heard it.

15

Keep it still

Knowledge and concepts

Early Learning Goals:
Use their imagination
Respond to music and enjoy what they hear

Concepts and other learning:
Reflect stillness through the body
Develop stamina in listening

Key vocabulary

feel   listen
still   imagine
time
slow

Resources and layout

▶ a small snippet of recorded music with a slow, reflective, drawn-out style – e.g. Barber's 'Adagio' or Albinoni's 'Adagio for strings'

▶ space for each child to lie down

Activity

1. **Show** the children how to raise their arm in a very slow movement until it's above their head and then lower it slowly down again.
2. **Do** the same while you play the snippet of music, raising and lowering one arm as the music plays.
3. **Now** all lie down on the floor.
4. **Tell** the children they can lie still and listen or move an arm very slowly as you play the music again.
5. **Leave** a pause at the end of the music, so they can be still and remember it in their heads. Fade the music to silence, don't turn it off abruptly.

and something else

✔ **Try** the same activity with both hands or start by bending down and slowly raising arms until they are standing with arms above their heads.

◆ Section 2

Body sounds

You can make music using anything at all as a sound source. It just has to be organised in a pattern, or repeated in different ways, and you can have music.

Activities in this section will help children to:

▶ explore the sounds and patterns they can make themselves with
   their hands
   their feet
   their mouth.

by doing things like...
   stamping
   tapping
   clapping
   rubbing
   hissing
   wiggling

...and lots more!

Hands

Knowledge and concepts

Early Learning Goals:
Express ideas using imaginative movement
Extend vocabulary and explore meaning

Concepts and other learning:
Understand that any movement makes a sound

Key vocabulary

bang	stroke
clap	repeat
slap	louder
tap	softer
rub	gentle

Resources and layout

▶ a quiet place and time

▶ sitting on the carpet

Activity

1. **Make** some tiny sounds with your hands and ask the children to copy them – e.g. stroke your hand on your sleeve or tap with your first finger only.

2. **Try** the same sounds with the other hand (right/left).

3. **Encourage** the children to find new sounds with their hands.

4. **Choose** some children to demonstrate their sounds.

5. **Find** words to describe the sounds, such as 'rough' 'quiet', and 'gentle'.

6. **Repeat** the best sounds to make patterns e.g. rub, rub, rub, rub, slap, slap, rub, rub, slap, slap, rubbadubba, rubbadubba.

and something else

✔ **Try** the same activity with louder sounds such as clapping, slapping and banging. Make some patterns with the sounds.

Feet

Knowledge and concepts

Early Learning Goals:
Move with confidence and safety
Explore sounds and meanings of new words

Concepts and other learning:
Understand that any movement makes a sound
Develop an interest in how instruments sound

Key vocabulary

jump   softer
bang   listen
heavy   stamp
loud   silent

Resources and layout

▶ standing up – preferably in the hall or another uncarpeted big space with a good echo

Activity

1. **Invent** some slow, heavy sounds the children can make with their feet.
2. **Everyone** moves around the space slowly and heavily, listening to the big sounds they are making.
3. **Now** find a slithery, sliding sound and do the same.
4. **Next,** everyone tries to find a tiny sound of their own and shares it with the group.
5. **See** if anyone can make some silent movements.
6. **Repeat** the best sounds lots of times to make a pattern, such as loud loud soft soft, or slither stamp stamp slither.

and something else

✔ **Find** words to describe the sounds and patterns, like 'heavy, noisy, fast, marching and cross'.

Mouths

Knowledge and concepts

Early Learning Goals:
Express ideas using imaginative movement
Extend vocabulary and explore meaning

Concepts and other learning:
Understand that musical patterns can come from repeating any sound
Develop good diction

Key vocabulary

hiss repeat
pop patterns
explode faster
listen slower

Resources and layout

▶ a quiet place and time
▶ sitting on the carpet

Activity

1. **Make** the sounds of the consonants as explosively as possible – 'p...', 'g...', 't...' etc.
2. **Repeat** them a lot to make patterns e.g. p-p-pooo/p-p-pooo/p-p-pooo or ch-ch-ch/ch-ch-ch or d-d-d-d, b-b-b-b, d-d-d-d, b-b-b-b.
3. **Help** children to find other ways to make sounds with their mouths e.g. finger popping and Red Indian noises.
4. **Try** some of them fast, slow or repeated in patterns.

and something else

✔ **Play** copycat with the noises, with individual children leading the others.

✔ **Find** words starting with the consonants they know. A little nonsense poem or rhyme might emerge. If it does, concentrate on the repeated patterns rather than any meaning e.g. p-p-poodle-poodle/ch-ch-chair/ch-ch-chair/b-b-bee etc.

Section 3

Using voices

The voice is the natural instrument for everyone and is particularly important for young children.

Be aware that children need a long time to develop their vocal chords to sing in tune. Because they can't yet sing in tune does not mean they can't hear or are not 'musical'.

Be very careful when singing with them to sing at a **high** enough pitch for their voices.

Activities in this section will help children to:

- ▶ develop vocal expression
- ▶ develop singing in tune
- ▶ learn lots of songs
- ▶ sing together in a community.

Sing lots of songs

If it is a regular, relaxed activity where the children do not feel self-conscious, singing is as natural as breathing. It should always take place in a positive, non-competitive atmosphere which reinforces a sense of community between the people in the group.

With young children, singing is best when:
- ▶ it is unaccompanied – music from a piano makes it harder, not easier, for children to hear their own voices and to get in tune;
- ▶ it is in a fairly narrow vocal range without big leaps. Take care with nursery rhymes such as Hot Cross Buns, which can be too difficult for most children (they were originally songs sung to children, not with them,;
- ▶ songs are sung at a reasonably high pitch, otherwise children find it hard find the notes and sing in tune;
- ▶ songs are learned by heart and by copying;
- ▶ songs are sometimes combined with movement;
- ▶ children stand up to sing, so they can breathe easily and produce a better sound;
- ▶ children stand close together for confidence.

More ways to help singing:
- ▶ do some choral speaking with a range of tones rather than a tune;
- ▶ sing the same song in different ways: very slowly, very softly, with eyes closed and very loudly (but not shouting);
- ▶ sing songs to sounds such as 'la', 'oo', 'ah', 'ee' etc.
- ▶ have two groups and sing a line each to encourage good listening;
- ▶ sing songs with actions or in different moods – happy or sad;
- ▶ let one group listen to another and comment on the singing;

▶ practice stopping and starting. Try a visual clue for stopping and starting – such as a puppet or hand sign;
▶ make sure that everyone knows the first note before starting the song.

Which songs should we sing?

Anything you and the children like and enjoy, but take care not to make the vocal range, leaps or vocabulary too difficult.

Don't forget the traditional songs entirely! The new versions are fun, but the old ones are tried and tested.

Try some of these as well as your own choices:

Traditional songs such as
Dance to Your Daddy
She'll be Coming Round the Mountain
Daisy, Daisy
Polly Put the Kettle on
Ring a Roses

Number and accumulative songs such as
One Man Went to Mow
One Potato, Two Potato
Old MacDonald
There's a Hole in My Bucket

Action and nonsense songs such as
Wind the Bobbin
If you're Happy and You Know it
I Went to the Animal Fair

Remember...

Some children have a wealth of songs they sing at home. Ask them to bring in a song they have learned at home, and teach it to the group. Your model will be the one children adopt. If your singing is apologetic, the children will produce a small sound; if your singing is bright and confident, the children's sound will be too!

Sing the register

Knowledge and concepts
Early Learning Goals:
Express and communicate ideas

Concepts and other learning:
Develop confidence in singing alone

Key vocabulary

hello days
good morning greetings
names

Resources and layout

▶ none in particular

Activity

1. **Start** with two notes only – like a playground chant or 'cuckoo'. Sing one note for each syllable and move between the two notes you have chosen. The child answers using your pattern and notes e.g.:

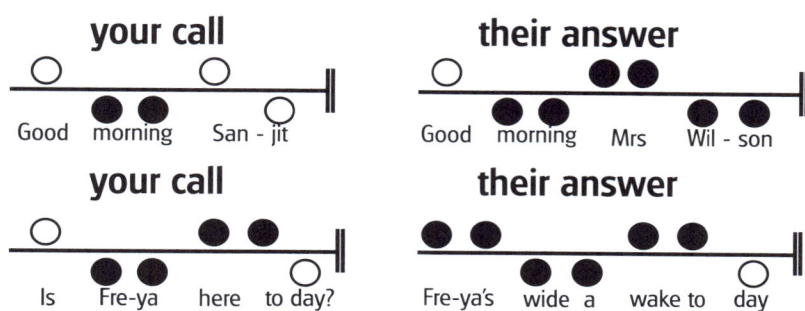

2. **Only** move on to a new call when they are used to the first one and can sing it mostly in tune.

and something else

✔ **Longer** conversations can be held and more notes used once the children have got the idea – such as 'Is your grandma better now?' – 'What's your baby brother called?'

N.B. keep the rhythm going. Make it like a real conversation.

Teddy Bear, Teddy Bear

Knowledge and concepts

Early Learning Goals:
Match movement to music

Concepts and other learning:
Opportunity to play an instrument individually

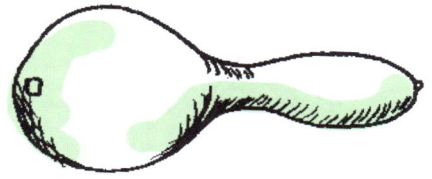

Key vocabulary

turn	gently
shake	tap
low	listen
high	hold

Resources and layout

▶ space to stand and move around

▶ a few percussion instruments or sound makers

Activity

The rhyme is:

Teddy Bear, Teddy Bear, turn around,
Teddy Bear, Teddy Bear, touch the ground,
Teddy Bear, Teddy Bear, climb the stairs,
Teddy Bear, Teddy Bear, say your prayers.

1. **Sing** the song/say the rhyme, putting in the appropriate actions.
2. **Now** choose sounds for each action e.g.
    turn around – shake maraccas
    touch the ground – tap claves or sticks
    climb the stairs – play low to high on a xylophone
    say your prayers – gently tap a triangle.
3. **Choose** children to play the sounds for each movement.

and something else

✔ **Try** playing the game again, with some of the children making the sounds behind a screen or cupboard. See if the others can guess the part of the rhyme being played.

Move along please

Knowledge and concepts

Early Learning Goals:
Explore and experiment with sounds and words
Work as part of a group

Concepts and other learning:
Add vocal or percussion sounds to a poem or song

Key vocabulary

action	chime bar
shakers	triangle
cymbals	drum
round and round	sounds

Resources and layout

▶ songs or poems – e.g. 'I Hear Thunder', 'The Wheels on the Bus'

▶ sitting on the carpet

Activity

1. **Sing** the song or say the poem until everyone knows it well from memory.
2. **Find** appropriate sounds to accompany the poem or song, such as taps on a drum, stroking a cymbal or tinging a triangle.
3. **Make** the sounds for each of the groups of people on the bus: shakers for the children, chopsticks for the grandmas' knitting and triangles for the lights etc.
4. **And** for I Hear Thunder – drums for the thunder, rainsticks or rattles for the rain and chime bars for 'I'm wet through'.

and something else

✔ **One** or two children play the sounds while everyone else sings.

✔ **Everyone** sings and plays instruments together (this is very hard and takes lots of practice!).

Choral speaking

Knowledge and concepts

Early Learning Goals:
Speak clearly and audibly
Sing simple songs from memory

Concepts and other learning:
Understand that choral speaking helps to develop variety in vocal tone

Key vocabulary

expression   pitch
light   mood
exaggerate
cross

Resources and layout

▶ a quiet place and time

▶ a short, light, amusing poem or verse that can be learned quickly – e.g. 'The Parrot' by Spike Milligan

Activity

Can a parrot eat a carrot
Standing on his head?
If I did that my mum would send me
Straight upstairs to bed.   (Spike Milligan)

1. **Learn** the poem until everyone knows it well and can say it rhythmically.
2. **Talk** about what it means (if anything). Discuss the mood – funny, amusing, silly – and how the children might exaggerate the words as they speak.
3. **Practice** exaggerated expression e.g. the voice going up for a question, heavy emphasis on 'If I...', a cross voice for 'straight upstairs to bed'.
4. **Perform** the verse together as a group, exaggerating pitch and expression. Try to make any listener laugh!

and something else

✔ **Try** choral speaking some other rhymes.

Tones

Knowledge and concepts

Early Learning Goals:
Recognise and explore how sounds change
Count reliably

Concepts and other learning:
To increase the range of vocal tone children can use to express themselves

Key vocabulary

tone	smooth
gentle	harsh
sweet	loud
cross	soft

Resources and layout

▶ sitting (possibly on the carpet but a larger space would also be good) with two children on chairs in front. Later all children must be able to sit opposite each other

Activity

1. **Everyone** practises counting together to five, ten or twenty.
2. **Discuss** how your voice changes when you are cross and when you are pleased. Demonstrate by, for example, saying some names in different ways and seeing if they can guess whether you are cross or pleased.
3. **An adult** and one child sit on their hands.
4. **They** count to ten, trying to sound cross in different ways e.g. very loudly, hissing or through clenched teeth. How many ways can they sound cross?
5. **With** another child, count sounding pleased.

and something else

✔ **All** children sit in pairs opposite one another and do the activity with each other.

✔ **Discuss** the various ways everyone managed to change the tone of their voices.

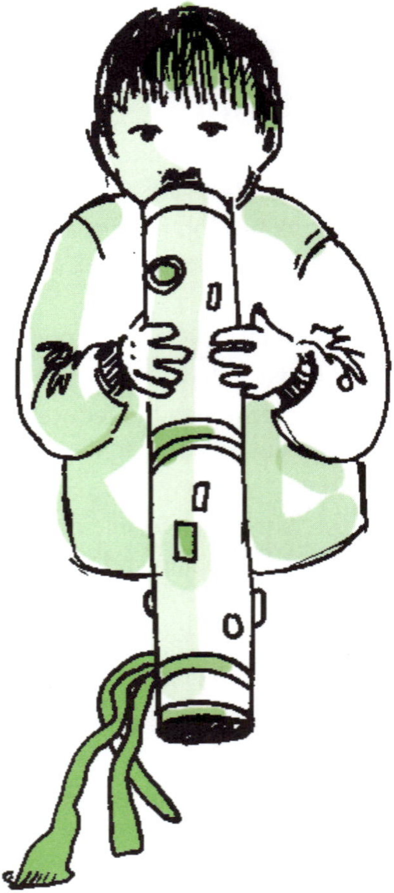

Section 4

Using other sound sources and instruments

Voices are the best and most immediate instruments to use with anyone, and especially young children, but a greater variety and more interesting musical colour can be had with the use of bought or homemade percussion instruments. Start with some common objects you will find near to hand such as keys, saucepans or garden sticks to develop rhythm and co-ordination.

Key things to remember when using instruments

- ✔ Good quality instruments made with good quality materials produce the most pleasing sounds. Buy the best you can afford.
- ✔ Have instruments close at hand to reduce the time lost in getting instruments out and putting them away.
- ✔ Noise is an inevitable part of music-making. From the start, manage the noise that will inevitably occur by using clear, well understood signals for stopping and starting, and expect an immediate response.
- ✔ Develop children's co-ordination skills so they can handle musical instruments confidently and well.
- ✔ Help children to respect the instruments and handle them with great care.
- ✔ Remember, your model is a powerful influence.

Activities in this section will help children to:

- ▶ make simple instruments
- ▶ develop co-ordination
- ▶ learn to control sound making
- ▶ explore sound qualities
- ▶ listen intently.

Making your own instruments

Good quality sound, like food, comes from using good ingredients or materials. However, you can make a useful start with these homemade, unpitched instruments.

Try some of these and let the children decorate them in their own way with paint, glitter and stickers etc.

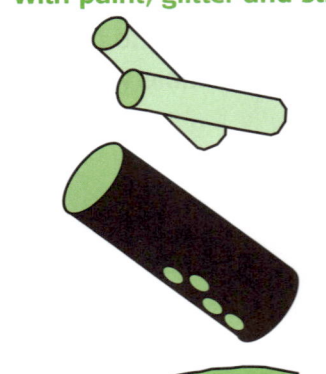

1. **Claves** – hard texture. Played in pairs. Cut dowel or broom handles into 20cm (8") lengths, and let the children help to sand them down and paint them.

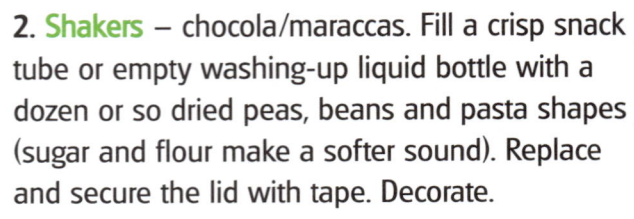

2. **Shakers** – chocola/maraccas. Fill a crisp snack tube or empty washing-up liquid bottle with a dozen or so dried peas, beans and pasta shapes (sugar and flour make a softer sound). Replace and secure the lid with tape. Decorate.

3. **Drums** – enclosed spaces which act as sound boxes. For example – a saucepan, a waste paper basket, a biscuit tin a washing-up bowl. Putting a lid on a plastic box drum improves the sound greatly.

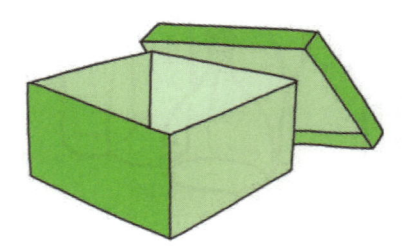

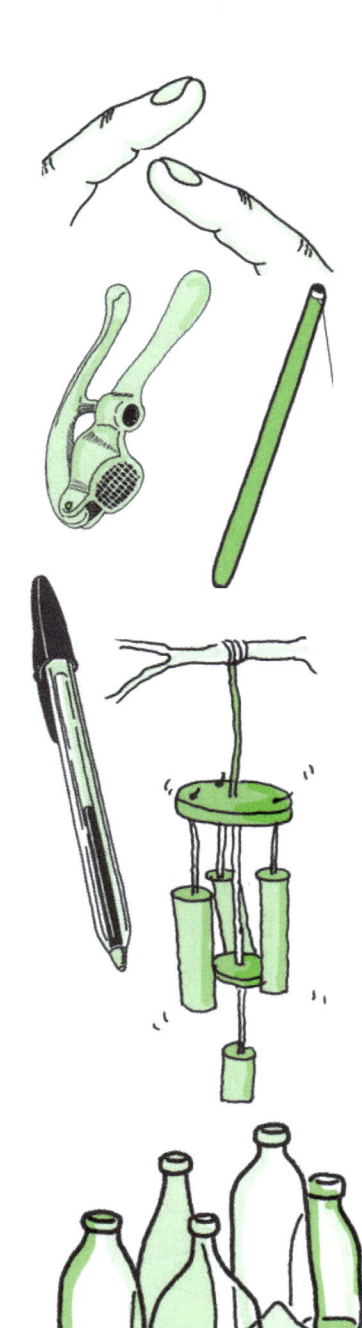

4. Beaters – make sure all beaters have smooth ends. Use wooden spoons, un-sharpened pencils, garden sticks or fingers.

5. Other ideas – a bunch of keys as shakers, garlic crusher as castanets and, a beater pulled along a radiator as a scraper. Moving anything at all makes a sound! Keep repeating the sound and you have a musical pattern.

6. Pitched percussion – Glasses and milk bottles do give you simple pitched instruments, but they are rather unsatisfactory, awkward to play and to get 'in tune'. The cheapest solution is to buy a set of eight chime bars and buy more when you can afford them.

Get co-ordinated

Knowledge and concepts

Early Learning Goals:
Move with control and co-ordination

Concepts and other learning:
Develop the co-ordination needed to play an instrument in time and feel a pulse

Key vocabulary

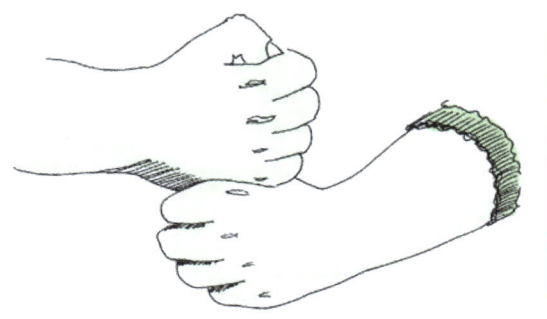

pulse   together
in time   repeat
left   rhythm
right

Resources and layout

▶ some activities need a carpet; some need a bigger space

Activity

Develop lots of small hand and finger control exercises through other activities such as dough, construction, threading and sorting.
Do some of these to a beat or in time, to help develop an inner pulse.

Try some of these to help with pulse and rhythm:

1. **Incy Wincy Spider.** Right hand thumb on left hand 1st finger, then left hand thumb to right hand 1st finger, to climb up the spout. Practice until perfect, then do the rhyme emphasising the rhythm as their fingers climb.
2. **Ears and nose.** Left hand 1st finger on nose, right hand 1st finger on right ear. Reverse to RH 1st finger on nose, LH 1st finger on left ear. Repeat lots of times in a rhythm.
3. **Marching to music.** Concentrate on feeling the left/right absolutely in time. Then repeat with left fist/right fist on their knees.
4. **One potato, two potato.** Clench fists on top of each other, and alternate the hands with each count. Do exaggerated movements to emphasise the pulse.
5. **Heads, shoulders, knees and toes.** Sing the song, using the actions to emphasise the rhythm.

N.B. There are more movement rhymes at the end of this book.

Let sleeping bells lie

Knowledge and concepts

Early Learning Goals:
Sustain attentive listening
Move with control

Concepts and other learning:
Understand that any small movement makes a sound
Develop the ability to make a very small sound

Key vocabulary

quiet	bells
still	tambourine
sleeping	careful
jingle	shake

Resources and layout

▶ sitting or standing in a circle

▶ instruments, such as bells or a tambourine, which make a sound with the smallest movement

Activity

1. **Show** the children how to make the jingling sound. Let several children (or all of them) have a go at jingling, so they understand the sound.
2. **Tell** the children that you are going to pass the bells or the tambourine around, but the jingles are sleeping and they must not be woken up!
3. **Pass** the instrument around the circle, trying not to jingle at all. Get everyone to listen for a jingle or the slightest sound.
4. **When** you've tried with one kind of instrument, have a go with another.

and something else

✔ **Try** the same activity with the bells or tambourine (or some keys) on the floor in the middle of the circle. Take turns to fetch the instrument and pass it to someone else without making a sound.

How long does it last?

Knowledge and concepts

Early Learning Goals:
Recognise how sounds can be changed
Recognise repeated sounds

Concepts and other learning:
Listen acutely and make judgements about the quality of a sound

long	short
ring	stop

Key vocabulary

long	listen
short	sound
ring	
stop	

Resources and layout

▶ instruments and household or classroom objects made from different materials e.g. a plastic box, wooden spoon, metal spoon, radiator, cymbal, wine glass or chime bar

▶ cards with words or symbols for long, short, ring, stop

Activity

1. **Play** some of the instruments and sound makers and listen for the sounds they make.
2. **When** the children have listened to some of the sounds, play a ringing sound e.g. a chime bar, bell or cymbal and ask the children to listen for when the sound stops.
3. **Next,** play two wooden spoons together and ask the same question.
4. **Talk** about long and short sounds and whether the sound rings (is a resonant sound) or stops quickly (a dead sound).
5. **Hold** up the 'long' and 'short' cards ask a child to choose a sound maker and make a single sound. The other children listen and point to the 'long' or 'short' card.

and something else

✔ **Sort** your sound makers into those that make short (dead) sounds and those that make long (resonant) sounds.

✔ **Make** some sound patterns e.g. 'short' 'short' 'long' 'long' **or** 'ring' 'ring' 'short' 'stop' 'ring' 'ring' 'stop' 'short'.

I went to market

Knowledge and concepts

Early Learning Goals:
Relate addition to combining groups of objects

Concepts and other learning:
Understand that any small movement makes a sound

Explore a range of sounds and collect them for future use

Key vocabulary

tambourine	piano
cymbal	chime bar
drum	triangle
high	castanets
low	shaker

Resources and layout

▶ a range of instruments and sound makers
▶ children sitting in a circle on the carpet

Activity

1. **If** the children don't know the game 'I went to market and bought a...', play it with groceries, toys or other shopping items first until they know how it works.
2. **When** they understand the format, play the game with musical sounds. Each child chooses a sound maker. They must say its sound as they play. For example:

Child 1: I went to market and bought a drum beat (plays drum beat)
Child 2: I went to market and bought a cymbal ting (plays cymbal)
Child 3: I went to market and bought a tambourine shake (plays tambourine)
Child 4: I went to market and bought a chime bar dong (plays chime)
Child 5: I went to market and bought a high note (plays on piano or sings high)

and something else

✔ **Try** the same activity cumulatively as each child adds something e.g. I went to market and bought a cymbal ting, a lion's roar, a triangle cling, and a drum beat. Each child plays the sound as they say the sequence.

What's different?

Knowledge and concepts

Early Learning Goals:
Communicate ideas, thoughts and feelings
Respond to what they hear

Concepts and other learning:
Develop musical memory and the ability to distinguish sounds and patterns of sounds

Key vocabulary

slow	sad
fast	jolly
loud	miserable
soft	different
cheerful	same

Resources and layout

▶ two very contrasting pieces of music (one minute for each) – e.g. loud and cheerful/slow and mournful; brass band fast and flashy/blues song; bouncy pop song/ballad or love song; jolly dance/slow dance

▶ children sitting on the carpet

Activity

1. **Play** one of the pieces (only about one minute). Talk about it using open questions such as: (What can you hear? What do you think they were feeling as they played the music? What does the music sound like).
2. **It's** a good idea to hear the piece more than once, maybe with some movements (see What a Character on page 14 before doing the next bit).
3. **Tell** the children to listen for what's different in the second piece. Play it once, and play it again. Talk about it using some more open questions such as: (What can you hear? What was different? What does it sound like now?)
4. **Use** the pieces again at quiet times during the next few days, perhaps when the children are coming in, during snack time or in the listening corner, so they get to know them really well.

and something else

✔ **Play** a bit more of the piece each time you use it, but always start at the beginning.

✔ **Always** tell them what the music is called.

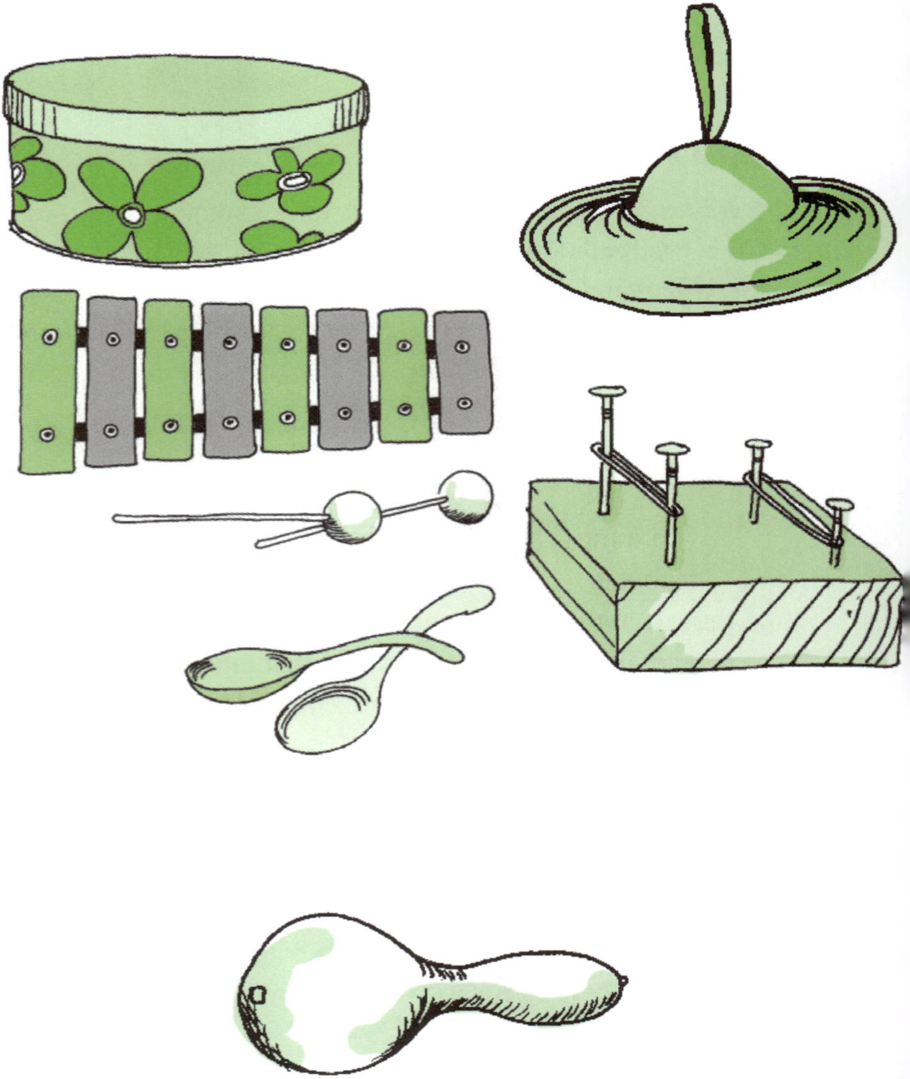

◆ Section 5

Patterns and numbers

When making music, it is common to repeat ideas and rhythms a lot, to use sets and patterns and to sing counting songs both upwards and downwards. In this way, children develop the ability to think in repeated units. Making musical patterns is very important in all music-making.

Activities in this section will help children to:

- ▶ find a musical idea, rhythm or sound
- ▶ repeat it
- ▶ repeat it again and again
- ▶ add another rhythm when the first one is going well, until you find you have a good tune or pattern.

Five green bottles

Knowledge and concepts
Early Learning Goals:
Sing a variety of songs from memory

Say and use number names in familiar contexts

Count back from five

Concepts and other learning:
Sing with other children

Key vocabulary

backwards   left
forwards   one less
listen   numbers 1 – 5
turn

Resources and layout

▶ children sitting on the carpet (at first), or standing (when the song is well known)

▶ five (ten when they can count backwards from ten) plastic water bottles (you could paint them green!)

Activity

1. **Learn** the first verse of Five Green Bottles slowly, by rote, making sure that it is pitched high enough for the children to be able to sing the notes.
2. **Talk** about the numbers going backwards.
3. **Now** sing all the verses, using the bottle props to help and pausing each time to count how many bottles are left.
4. **Count** the bottles remaining each time until the children know
    the sound really well.
5. **When** the children can sing Five Green Bottles, let them take turns to remove a bottle for each verse and count how many are left.
6. **When** they are ready, progress to Ten Green Bottles.

and something else

✔ **This** game also works with Ten in the Bed (try with soft toys under a blanket), or One Man Went to Mow (with children in a row).

Do it again

Knowledge and concepts

Early Learning Goals:

Practice turn taking

Recognise repeated sound and patterns

Know that in English and in music we read from left to right

Concepts and other learning:

Symbols can be used for sounds

Key vocabulary

long	pattern
short	repeat
loud	more
soft	less

Resources and layout

▶ three instruments or sound sources (e.g. tambourine, shaker, bells and chime bar)

▶ flash cards with pictures of each (several for each instrument, large and small sizes)

Activity

1. **Spend** some time looking at the instruments and experimenting with the sounds they make.
2. **Practice** playing each one loudly, quietly, for a long time, for a short time, making a pattern with them.
3. **When** the children are familiar with the instruments, show them the flash cards, naming each picture and talking about the sizes of the pictures.
4. **Lay** out three cards the same size and ask three children to play as you point to each one.
5. **Lay** out the same three cards plus one small one and see whether the children can play loud and soft as you point to the cards.
6. **Now** let the children experiment and make patterns to play themselves or for other children to play.

and something else

✔ **Leave** this activity in a quiet area so the children can play the game on their own. Give them some blank cards too.

Birds, beasts and butterflies

Knowledge and concepts
Early Learning Goals:
Use their imagination and respond to experiences

Know that in English and in music we read from left to right

Concepts and other learning:
Develop understanding of simple symbols for sounds

Key vocabulary

low	slow
heavy	fast
deep	high
large	light

Resources and layout

▶ large cards with pictures of animals, birds and butterflies
▶ a range of sound makers (castanets, triangle, drum, scrapers, bells, including very large/low sounds e.g. low notes on a piano, keyboard, drum or guitar)

Activity

1. **Make** some birds, beasts and butterflies cards (you could get the children to draw the pictures).
2. **Look** at each card and talk about the creatures. Talk about the sort of sound each would make. How big is it? How does it move? Can it fly? Is it scary?
3. **Choose** two cards for the session (perhaps an elephant and a butterfly).
4. **Decide** on instruments and voice sounds for each e.g. low drums and trumpet sounds played very slowly for an elephant; triangles or bells played very fast for butterflies.
5. **Two** groups of children play and make sounds for each picture, repeating them lots of times.
6. **Now** try with each group playing when their sign is up and stopping when it isn't.

and something else

✔ **Leave** the cards in your music corner for the children to use on their own. Add some blank cards for their own ideas.

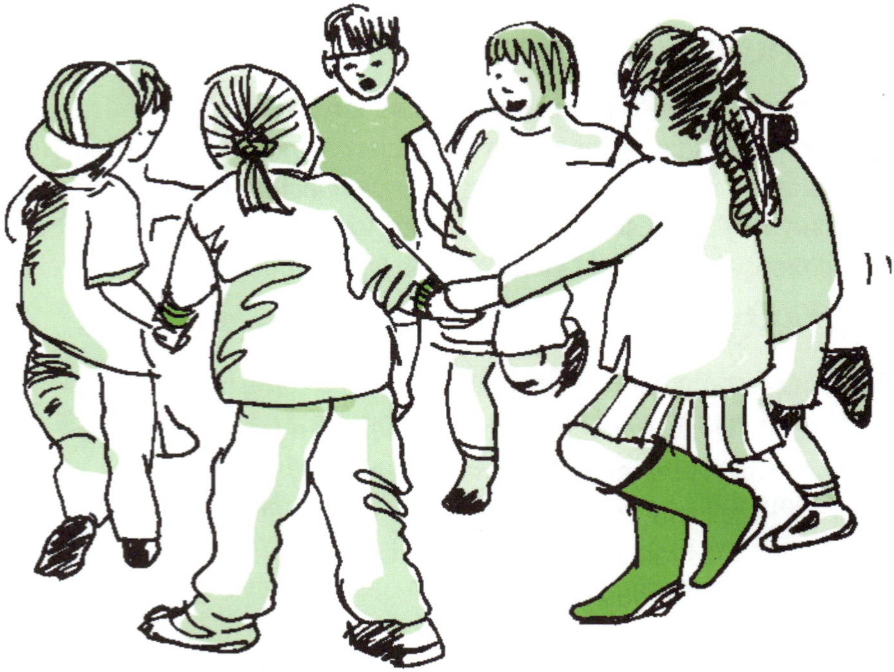

Section 6

Rhymes and stories

Pattern making encourages thinking about music as an abstract activity. Working with stories and words gives another context for music and provides an excellent framework for experiment and imagination. Trails provide a valuable structure for inventing musical stories. When the structure is understood, you can go anywhere and make a musical picture as a memory of your visit.

Activities in this section will help children to:

- ▶ reinforce the rhythmic link between music and words
- ▶ feel the pulse of rhymes
- ▶ explore sound qualities through words
- ▶ illustrate stories with sounds
- ▶ make musical stories.

What's your name again?

Knowledge and concepts

Early Learning Goals:

Make up their own rhymes

Explore and experiment with sounds and words

Concepts and other learning:

Make simple rhythms and sound patterns

Key vocabulary

rhyme   repeat
pattern   rhythm

Resources and layout

▶ no additional resources
▶ a quiet place and time, children sitting on the carpet

Activity

1. **Talk** to the children about the sounds and rhythms of their own names.
2. **Talk** about other people's names and look at ones that rhyme e.g. Sam/Pam, Ron/Jon, Millie/Jilly, Karen/Sharon.
3. **Repeat** a name over and over and put it in a pattern:
   Daisy, Daisy, Daisy,   Kishan, Kishan,
   Daisy, Daisy, Doh.   or   Kishan, Kishan, Go!
4. **Use** several names to make a rhythm or rhyme:
   Murali, Giri, Jimmy and Joe
   Ella and Lana and Freya and Mo.
5. **Sing** the rhymes in little tunes, repeating each line until it ceases to sound like the names.
6. **Add** a simple beat on a tambourine or claves (sticks) to keep the rhythm going.

and something else

✔ **Groups** of children could make up their own rhymes, then 'perform' them to each other. It's important to practise it several times before performing it to someone.

Grandfather, father and son

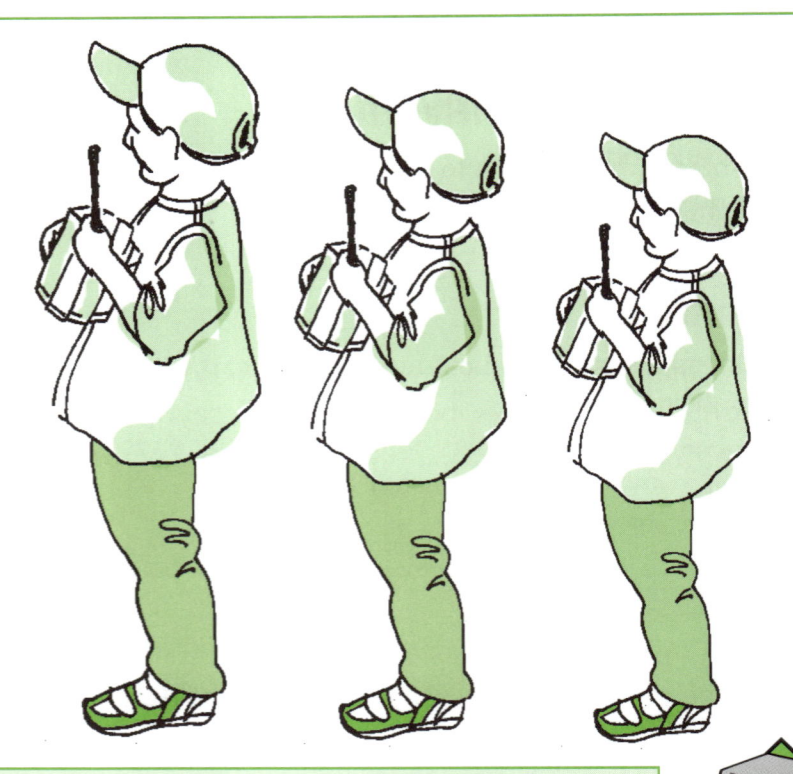

Knowledge and concepts

Early Learning Goals:

Respond with enjoyment to rhymes and poems

Use their imagination in music and stories

Concepts and other learning:

To feel different speeds and moods and convey them through movement

Key vocabulary

slowly	speed up
faster	slow down
hurry	stop
beat	start
in time	

Resources and layout

- a big space with room to move
- a drum
- the rhyme already learned by heart

Activity

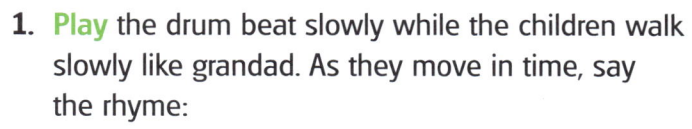

1. **Play** the drum beat slowly while the children walk slowly like grandad. As they move in time, say the rhyme:

    Slowly, slowly walks my grandad,
    Leaning hard upon his stick,
    Wait for me, my dear, says grandad,
    'I'm too old, I can't be quick'.

2. **Speed** up the drum beat – and ask who is walking now? As the children move faster, say this bit of the rhyme:

    Father goes to work each morning,
    This is how **he** walks along.

3. **Speed** up the drum beat – and ask who is walking now? As the children move faster, say this bit of the rhyme:

    Off to school I have to hurry,
    Going down the road **I** run.

and something else

- ✔ **Make** up another poem about grandma, mum and me.
- ✔ **Use** other instruments to vary the sound for each character in the poem (triangle, tambourine and xylophone).

Animal fair

Knowledge and concepts
Early Learning Goals:
Express ideas using imaginative movement

Match movements to music

Explore and experiment with sounds and words

Concepts and other learning:
Words and phrases will convert into rhythms

Key vocabulary

rhythm	actions
rhyme	in time
repeat	accompaniment
verse	beat

Resources and layout

▶ children sitting on the carpet with space to play instruments
▶ the 'Animal Fair' song
▶ 'soft' instruments such as claves, chime bars and bells

Activity

1. **Learn** the words and the song:

The Animal Fair
'I went to the animal fair, all the birds and the beasts were there,
The big baboon by the light of the moon was combing his auburn hair,
The monkey fell out of his bunk, and slid down the elephant's trunk,
The elephant sneezed and fell on his knees,
But what became of the monkey, monkey, monkey...'

2. **Think** of some actions for parts of the song e.g. 'birds and beasts' or 'fell on his knees'. Practice the song and movements until the children know them well.
3. **Now** try repeating 'monkey, monkey, monkey,' as a rhythm. If there are two adults, try singing in two groups, with one group singing 'monkey, monkey' while the others sing the verse.
4. **Try** playing the 'monkey, monkey' rhythm on claves or a chime bar as the children sing the song.
5. **Let** children take turns to play the accompaniment, helping them to keep in time.

and something else

✔ **For** older children, try the same activity with the children clapping or slapping their knees as they sing.

N.B. Playing instruments, beat work, clapping, stamping and walking all use both sides of the brain and help with learning.

Peace at last!

Knowledge and concepts

Early Learning Goals:

Use their imagination and respond to stories

Explore sounds and words

Concepts and other learning:

Begin to develop a sense of sequence, structure and performance

Key vocabulary

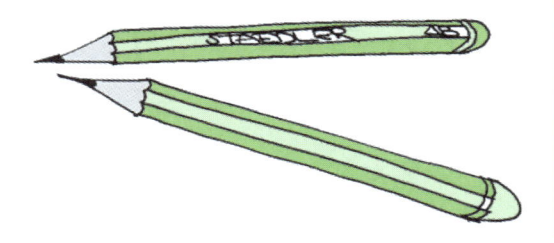

sound   high
effect   loud
perform   soft
low

Resources and layout

▶ 'Peace at Last' by Jill Murphy (or another story with repetitive elements and opportunities for making sounds
▶ a variety of sound makers
▶ children sitting on the carpet or in a circle of chairs

Activity

1. **Read** the story to the children.
2. **Talk** about the bits of the story that suggest sound effects, and get them to suggest which sounds would fit.
3. **Pick** a few key parts of the story, gather your sounds, practice them and discuss how they work. For example:
   Going to bed – a xylophone or piano played slowly, low to high
   Snoring – a scraper, or vocal snoring sounds
   Clock – pencil or claves tapped together
   Walking – fingers tapped on the floor
   Owl – vocal owl hoot
   Birds – bells shaken gently
   Alarm – bells played loudly and whole group 'drrringgg'.
4. **Agree** who is making which sound effect and when.
5. **Read** the story again and 'perform' with sound effects.

and something else

✔ **Find** an audience for your story with sound effects – another class or group or some parents.

Goldilocks

Knowledge and concepts

Early Learning Goals:
Respond to stories and explore sounds

Concepts and other learning:
To add vocal sounds and instruments to enhance a story
Develop the ability to hear higher and lower sounds

Key vocabulary
repeat pitch
high tone of voice
low names of instruments

Resources and layout

- the story of Goldilocks
- a range of instruments and sounds suitable for the key elements in the story

Activity

Some examples of sounds to try:

The forest - vocal sounds of wind in trees or birds twittering

The three bowls – three pitched wood blocks (or bowls and spoons?)

The three chairs – three pitched triangles or chimes, getting higher

The three beds – three pitched shakers or piano notes

The three bears – speaking in three different voices or pitches

Goldilocks – could have a tune on chime bars, specially for her.

1. **Read** the story of Goldilocks and discuss the tone of voice used to indicate the three bears and their different sizes.
2. **Discuss** the different pitches and what would be good to use for each bear, bowl chair etc.
3. **Decide** who is going to play, what and when. Practice the parts where the sounds come.
4. **Read** the story through again with the sounds played by the children in a 'performance'.

and something else

✔ **Find** an audience of other children for an informal concert.

73

Story Trails

Knowledge and concepts

Early Learning Goals:

Develop an understanding of story sequence

Concepts and other learning:

To use a simple musical structure
Begin to develop control of sounds and patterns of sounds in sequence

Resources and layout

▶ large white board or paper on an easel or flip chart
▶ a range of instruments and sound makers
▶ children in a circle

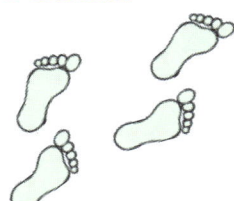

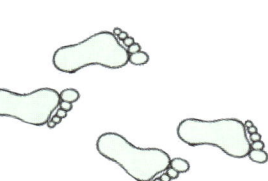

We went to the park and we saw...

a dog barking

a motor bike

Key vocabulary
sound
character
musical picture
sequence
low

regular
jumpy
smooth
high

birds singing

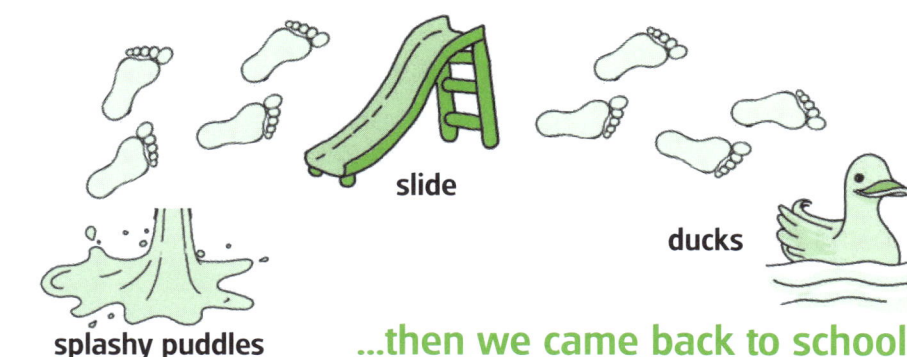

splashy puddles

slide

ducks

...then we came back to school

75

Activity

1. **Decide** on somewhere to visit for your musical trail or use a recent visit to the park, the zoo or the shops.
2. **Talk** about the bits they liked best e.g. the monkeys at the zoo, splashing in the puddles at the park the electric doors at the shops.
3. **Decide** on some sounds and sound makers for the favourite bits. Don't forget voice and body sounds! For example:
   The monkeys – vocal noises or a bouncy drum
   The puddles – a cymbal
   The doors – running a beater up a xylophone or voice 'swooooshes'.
4. **Decide** who will make the walking sound as the trail goes on (slapping on thighs, beat on a drum etc).
5. **Try** out the sounds. Decide who will play them and when.
6. **Draw** the map on the big board, with pictures for each sound. Follow the trail with a pointer. The children play their sounds when the pointer reaches their picture.

and something else

✔ **Choose** somewhere else to visit and make up a different musical picture.

✔ **Leave** the trail out so children can play on their own.

Additional Resources

Each activity should be self-sufficient but when you have tried them you may want to explore further the use of other recorded music or instruments.

Using recorded music
Use anything you like. It is important that you communicate delight in the music yourself so it's best to know it quite well before you use it. Make sure that children hear a range of different moods and styles. Limit the extracts you use to no more than a minute each, but be aware of the need to build up children's stamina for listening too. Play what you play on lots of different occasions so that they get to know it quite well. Give it a name too so they can identify it and ask, 'When are we going to hear "xxx" again'?

Other resources
This is not meant to be a comprehensive list, just a short indication of some resources that will provide you with an excellent bank of music ideas and theoretical support for early years.

The Red Pack of Music Materials for Early Years is a comprehensive and easy to use collection of 80 activities, some long, some short, along with a scheme of work closely related to the Early Learning Goals. It also contains a substantial and useful booklist.
Published by Leicestershire Music Publications. The Red Pack is available from Featherstone Education and available at a special price to purchasers of The 'Little Book of Music'.

Gently into Music
Progressive activities into Key Stage 1.
Published by Longman.

Playsongs
Games and songs for babies, toddlers and very young children.
Published by Playsongs.

Music in the Early Years
Textbook for early years teachers of music, with practical examples.
Published by Falmer.

Small Voices, Big Noises
CD of music to use with pre-school children.
Published by Featherstone Education, an imprint of A&C Black. Available at a special price to purchasers of 'The Little Book of Music'.

Continuity and progressio[n]

The **Baby & Beyond**™ series takes simp[le] activities or resources and shows how they can [be] used with children at each of the EY[FS] development stages, from birth to 60+ mont[hs]. Each double page spread covers one activity, [so] you can see the progression at a glance.

Shows how simp[le] resources can be us[ed] by children at differe[nt] ages and stag[es]

Inspiration for planning continuous provision

Messy Play	978-1-905019-58-8
The Natural World	978-1-905019-57-1
The Sensory World	978-1-905019-60-1
Sound and Music	978-1-905019-59-5
Mark Making	978-1-905019-78-6
Construction	978-1-905019-77-9
Dolls & Soft Toys	978-1-905019-80-9
Bikes, Prams, Pushchairs	978-1-905019-76-2
Role Play	978-1-906029-02-9
Finger Play & Rhymes	978-1-906029-01-2
Dens & Shelters	978-1-906029-03-6
Food	978-1-906029-04-3

To see the full range of Featherstone books visit www.acblack.co[m]

hrough the EYFS

Great for the Early Years Foundation Stage!

Ideal to support progression and extend learning.

Baby & Beyond™ — progression in play for babies and children

- Food & Cooking (NEW)
- Dens & Shelters (NEW)
- Mark Making
- Bikes, Prams & Pushchairs
- Dolls & Soft Toys
- The Natural World
- Construction
- The Sensory World
- Play
- Sound and Music
- Finger Play & Rhymes
- Messy Play

The Little Books Club

Little Books meet the need for exciting and practical activities which are fun to do, address the Early Learning Goals and can be followed in most settings. As one user put it ,

> 'When everything else falls apart I know I can reach for a Little Book and things will be fine!'

We publish ten Little Books a year – one a month except for August and December. Little Books Club members receive each new Little Book on approval at a reduced price as soon as it is published.

Examine the book at your leisure. Keep it or return it. You decide.

That's all. No strings. No joining fee. No agreement to buy a set number of books during the year. And you can leave at any time.

Little Books Club members receive:

- ✔ each new Little Book on approval as soon as it's published
- ✔ a specially reduced price on that book and on any other Little Books they buy
- ✔ a regular, free newsletter dealing with club news and aspects of Early Years curriculum and practice
- ✔ free postage on anything ordered from our catalogue
- ✔ a discount voucher on joining which can be used to buy from our catalogue
- ✔ at least one other special offer every month.

There's always something in Little Books to help and inspire you!

Phone: 0207 440 2446   Email: littlebooks@acblack.com